Myra Brooks-Turner Piano Duo Collection

Yankee Doodle Duo
Op. 75 No. 2

(2 Pianos - 4 Hands)

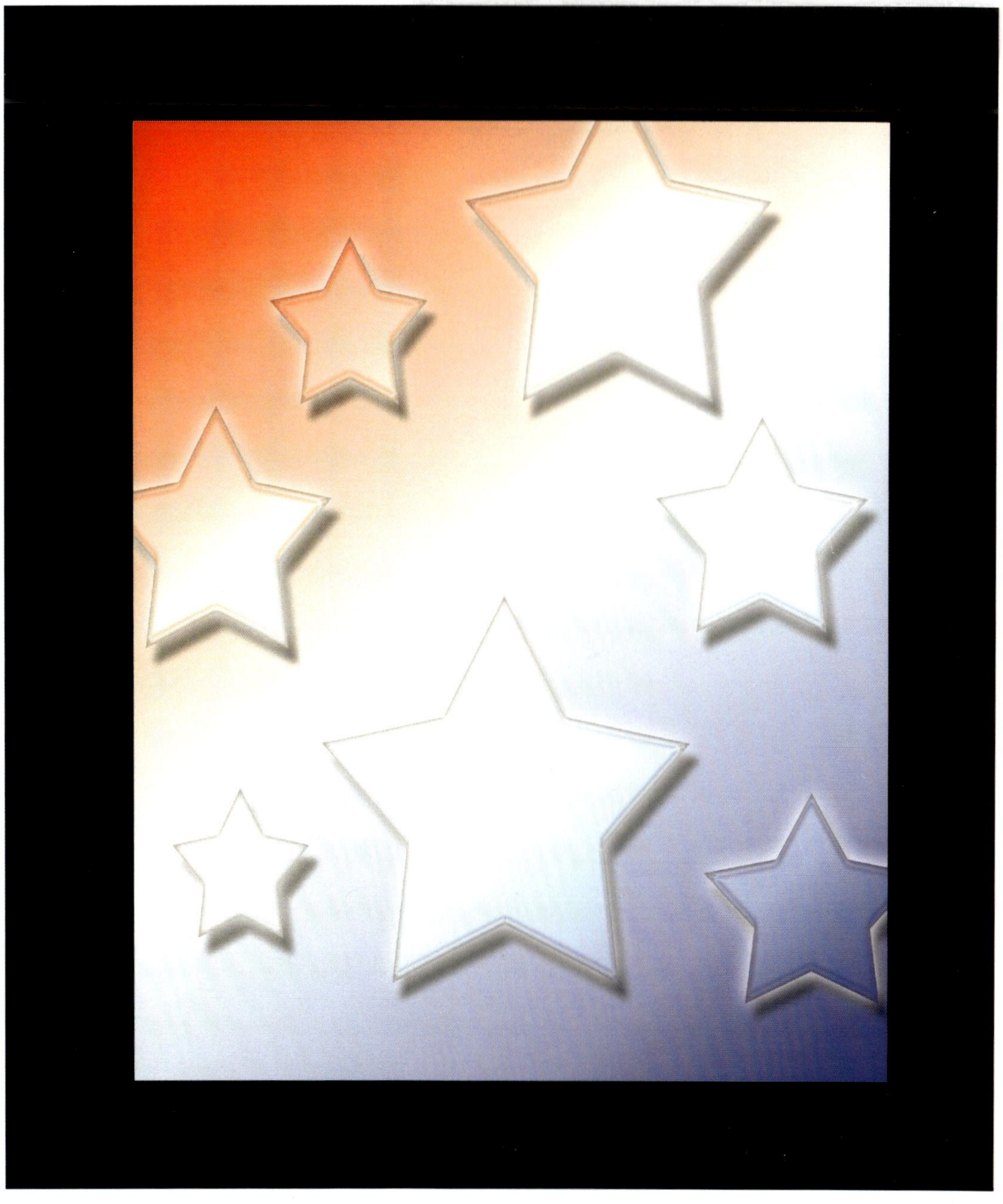

71-13

Yankee Doodle Duo

To Dr. Christopher David Sarzen

Improvisation by
Myra Brooks-Turner, Op. 75 No. 2
Themes by George M. Cohan and John Philip Sousa

Schaum Publications, Inc.
10235 N. Port Washington Rd.
Mequon, WI 53092
www.schaumpiano.net

Level Six

ISBN 978-1-62906-015-6

7113 $3.99 in USA

EXCLUSIVELY
DISTRIBUTED BY
HAL LEONARD

00645843
U.S. $3.99